Stress-Free

Children's Parties

AMANDA MUDEN

INDEX

Published in 1995 by Merehurst Limited

Ferry House, 51-57 Lacy Road, Putney, London SW15 1PR

Distributed by J B Fairfax Press Limited, 9 Trinity Centre, Park Farm,

Wellingborough, Northants, NN8 6ZB

Reprinted 1995

ISBN 1-85391-415-0 (cased)

ISBN 1-874567-47-6 (paperback)

A catalogue record of this book is available from the British Library.

Managing Editor: Barbara Croxford
Designed by Bill Mason
Photography: Jon Bouchier and Daniel Pangbourne
Illustrations by Sarah Harmer

Colour separation by Fotographics Ltd UK-Hong Kong
Printed and bound in Barcelona, Spain by Cronion, S.A.

CONTENTS

Who, What, When and Where?

Party time is fast approaching and the thought of an army of excitable children on your hands sends you into a state of sheer terror. Well, push your fears aside and start at the beginning.

Who to Invite
• • • •

The first thing you need to decide is who you are going to invite. Are you going to invite your children's friends who are all in the same age group? Or, are you going to include family as well, making the ages very varied. If you do decide to invite a wide age range, beware – you are making a lot of work for yourself. The activities that appeal to an eight-year old will completely go over the head of a four-year old. Unless you are extremely well prepared you have a potential nightmare on your hands! (see *Troubleshooting* on page 66).

Also, be realistic about the number of children you feel you can manage.

Invitations
• • • •

There is a wide variety of children's party invitations readily available in most card and party shops. However, it is cheaper and much more fun if you and your child make the invitations together.

The simplest way to do this is to buy plain postcards and a small pack of children's brightly coloured stickers. Ask your child to draw a picture on the front of each postcard with wax crayons and add a sticker to the back of the card. Then you simply address the card, add the time, date, place, your child's name and age. You must also make sure that you add *RSVP* to your invitations as this will help with the catering and party bags. Send out the invitations about two-to-three weeks before the party day. Don't send them out any earlier as they tend to get lost, and if you send them out too late the children could be booked up.

Where to have the Party
• • • •

This is a fairly big decision – you need to take into account how many children you are going to have, what age the children are, how many adults there are going to be, and what sort of party you want.

☆ Home: this is nearly always the best place to have a party. The children feel comfortable with the surroundings,

one of these places exclusively is going to cost a fair amount of money.

Wherever you decide to have the party, make sure that you organize a separate area for eating, away from the main entertainment. It can also double up as an area for the adults to congregate in.

When to have the Party
● ● ● ●

If you are going to have the party at home, you can choose the time and day, but if you are going to hire somewhere, you may have to be more flexible.

If the children are fairly young, then earlier in the day is best. Older children prefer later in the day, especially if you are having a disco party. If you are going to hire somewhere, book it as soon as you set your date – it's amazing how quickly they get booked up.

everything you need is close to hand, you don't have to worry about packing endless bags and boxes, and you certainly don't have to worry about booking the venue weeks in advance.

☆ Hall: most of us have a community hall nearby. Generally, they are fairly well equipped and comply with safety regulations. They are usually cheap to hire and fairly good for parking.

☆ Hotel: this option is a lot more expensive, though a hotel will normally supply a complete package. If you do have the budget for it, this certainly is the best way to have a stress-free party.

☆ Local park: if you don't have a garden, you can take the children to the local park for a great summer-time party. Make sure that you have enough adult helpers around as you don't want to lose anybody!

☆ Recreational centres/sports clubs/ leisure centres/swimming pools: to hire

Forward Planning
● ● ● ●

Good forward planning is the key to a stress-free party; follow the guidelines on page 12 and you will have no trouble. The important thing is to know exactly what you are doing and how to do it. Nothing is worse than trying to organize children to play a game that you don't know how to play yourself; they will run riot as you limp through the instructions.

Included in this book are full party plans for all age ranges. In each party plan I have included an activity for the children as soon as they arrive. This will relax them and allow any latecomers to settle in and not feel too awkward. Each party plan is arranged so that there are quiet games before tea – to calm everyone and stop any wild behaviour at the tea table – and more of the same immediately afterwards to stop the children dancing on a full stomach!

The Party Countdown on page 12 will ensure you have everything you need for

Spotty Dotty alias the author!

any party and then there is an additional checklist for each age group.

Party Prop Box

It is essential to prepare a party prop box with everything you need to entertain the children inside it.

Helpers
• • • •

It is always advisable to enlist some helpers, but make sure that you prime them first as to what you would like them to do. Try not to have too many as this tends to intimidate the children and if there is not enough for them to do they usually start chatting and become more of a hindrance than a help! In my experience, two helpers are plenty.

Decorations
• • • •

Decorations create a fun atmosphere, putting everyone in the right frame of mind, but don't go overboard because they

take too much time and energy and create too much temptation for the children.

Balloons, streamers and the odd touch to enhance a theme are usually enough. Bring out the Christmas tree lights for added atmosphere.

Professional Entertainers
• • • •

A good, professional children's entertainer will definitely make a party stress-free. It may seem expensive but good entertainers are worth their weight in gold. Be wary if someone is extremely cheap. It means that they probably won't have much in the way of props and costumes, and your party will suffer!

Make sure you give the entertainer all the party details; the name of the birthday child, the age of the children, how many, date, time and place of the party. In fact, to put your mind at rest, make sure that they confirm in writing. Check exactly what they are going to do. The majority of entertainers will gladly run the whole party for you, providing games, music and fun before tea and a full show afterwards. This leaves you with only the tea to worry about. Alternatively, you can hire an entertainer simply to give a complete show after tea.

The following types of entertainment are usually offered by entertainers:

★ Magic
★ Puppets
★ Drama workshop parties
★ Face painting
★ Balloon modelling
★ Ventriloquism
★ Discos
★ Storytelling
★ Juggling
★ Plate spinning
★ Karaoke

If you decide to book a magician make sure he/she is a member of the Magic Circle and you will be guaranteed a good show. (See also page 71.)

Party Games

The following are some of the best-loved and well-known party games. They are played differently for each age group (see the individual chapters).

Try to keep the pace moving in each game. If the children start to get bored, move it along a bit quicker or go on to another activity. With any of the elimination games like *Musical Bumps* tell the players who are out that they are judges. This stops them feeling like failures and keeps their interest in the game. With any of the team games, make sure that you have at least one other adult helping you.

Don't make too much distinction between winners and losers. It is better if everyone gets something, however small. As a rule, children are very competitive and feel miserable if they don't win anything!

Name Game
• • • •

For this game you will need some stickers for writing the children's names on, a marker pen and a whistle or something that makes a funny noise. Get the children to sit in a circle and ask them to count to four, clapping their hands at the same time.

After each count of four, blow the whistle, point to all the children in turn, ask them their name, and give them a sticker with their name on.

Pass the Parcel
• • • •

Wrap up a small prize in several layers of paper and sticky tape. Between each layer put a sweet or a forfeit. This should be

Sleeping lions is good for calming things down.

organized well before the start of the party! The players sit in a circle, music is played and the parcel is passed around. As the music stops, the person holding the parcel removes a layer. This continues until some-one reaches the small prize. If you are giving out sweets make sure there are enough for everyone or tears may result.

Musical Bumps
••••

Music plays and the partygoers either dance or jump up and down. When the music stops they have to bump down onto the floor. The last one to bump down becomes a judge and this carries on until only one person is left.

Islands
••••

Each player is given an 'island' (either a postcard or a postcard-sized piece of card or paper). The children find a space and stand on their islands. When the music starts the players either walk, dance, or skip around the room. While the music is playing the children are not allowed to tread on the islands but, as soon as the music stops, the children have to stand on the nearest one. Only one player per island is allowed and they must stand on different islands every time. Each time the music stops, an island is taken away. Anyone who doesn't have an island becomes a judge. The last person left on an island is the winner.

Musical Statues
••••

The music plays and everyone dances. When the music stops everyone has to stand as still as a statue. Anyone who moves becomes a judge.

Sleeping Lions
••••

This is my favourite game! Whenever you want to calm things down a bit, this is the one to choose. The children have to lie on the floor without making a sound or moving a muscle. I always count to ten then look around to see who is the stillest, quietest person at the party. If they are really good at keeping still, you can start little tricks such as calling out 'Teatime', 'There is a big spider crawling across the room' or 'Who wants a sweetie?' With younger children, I always get them to roar and move around the room like a lion. With older ones, you can leave them there for hours!

Flap the Fish
• • • •

This can be an individual contest or a team relay race. If played as an individual contest, you will need one folded newspaper and one large paper fish per player. Using tissue paper, cut out large fish shapes and ask your child to decorate them. For a relay race, you need one fish/paper set per team.

Each player is required to drive their fish over a pre-determined course by fanning behind it with the newspaper.

Agadoo
• • • •

Most record shops will stock this song. All you need to do is listen to the lyrics and make up some actions to go with them. Start with everyone standing in a circle.

Bubblegum
• • • •

Everyone sits in a circle. The birthday child starts off by chewing some imaginary bubblegum. They have a good old chew. Then they take it out of their mouth and do something really horrible to it, rub it in their hair, stick it up their nose and then pass it on. The next person then has to start the imaginary chewing, pretending to feel ill knowing what has been done to the chewing gum before. Carry on until everyone has had a go.

Chinese Whispers
• • • •

Sit all the children in a circle. The birthday child thinks of a sentence to whisper into their neighbour's ear. They in turn must pass the message on. The last person to receive it must stand up and say what they have heard. The children can only repeat the message once. You will be suprised how the sentence changes.

Countdown to the Party

One month before the party
· · · · ·

★ Decide when to have the party
★ Where?
★ Book a hall if you need to (you may need more time than a month)
★ Book an entertainer if you need to (again you may need more than a month)
★ Decide who to invite
★ Order the cake (if you need to)
★ Make or buy invitations

Three weeks before the party
· · · · ·

★ Send out the invitations

Two weeks before the party
· · · · ·

★ Buy the decorations: balloons, streamers, tinsel, any decorations to aid your theme
★ Buy the party tableware: plates, napkins, tablecloth, plastic cutlery and cups
★ Plan the menu
★ Organize your child's costume or clothing
★ Tape the music for the party

One week before the party
· · · · ·

★ Check the guest list – Who is coming?
★ Buy the party prizes
★ Buy the goodies for the party bags
★ Make or buy the cake
★ Check that you have candles and matches for the cake
★ Check the booking if you are hiring somewhere
★ Check the booking if you are hiring an entertainer
★ Put film in the camera
★ Organize sticky labels

Four days before the party
· · · · ·

★ Organize a party prop box - each age group should have the following items inside:
★ Party prizes
★ Music/cassettes and something to play them on
★ Sticky name labels
★ Party plan
Additional items needed for each age range are listed in the appropriate chapters.

Two days before the party
· · · · ·

★ Check the cake
★ Do the food shopping (don't forget the adults)

The day before the party
· · · · ·

★ Check you have all the food you need
★ Prepare the food as much as possible
★ Check the party prop box
★ Get the party bags ready

The day of the party
· · · · ·

If at home:
★ Check the house is ready, with breakable and any potentially dangerous objects out of the way, not too many toys around, pets out of the way, an adults' area
★ Put up decorations
★ Lay out food tables
★ Candles on the cake, sharp knife
★ Party prop box ready
★ Party bags ready for action
★ Music at the ready
★ Balloons on the door.

3 year olds and under
Fairies and Elves

At-a-Glance Party Plan

Colouring station

Story with actions

Name Game

Ring-a-Ring o' Roses

The Farmer's in his Den

Pass the Parcel

Musical Bumps

Sleeping Lions

Teatime

Puppets

Hokey-cokey

The Wheels on the Bus

Here we go round the Mulberry Bush

Stand-up spot

Lucky Dip or Going-home Bags

The three-and-under age-range is the most difficult group to keep entertained, the main reason being that they don't really want to be! When they arrive they will most certainly be escorted by a parent or nanny who may be reluctant to leave them. So here lies your first problem – grown-ups, who, as a rule, seem to go into 'not too helpful' mode at other children's parties. The main problem with grown-ups is that they tend to talk louder than you, whilst you are desperately trying to get the children's attention. The last thing you want to do with this age group is raise your voice, as you will frighten the children.

Another problem with grown-ups being around is that some children tend to cling to them and this really stops the children joining in. The best way to avoid this problem is to set up a special area for the adults. Delegate a friend to look after them, making sure they have enough food and drink

and see what actions you can use. For instance The *Three Little Pigs* is a great story to start with. When the wolf knocks at the door you can get everybody knocking with him. Get them to join in with 'I'll huff and I'll puff and I'll blow your house down'. This will get everybody participating.

Name Game
••••

For this game you will need some stickers with all the children's names on. Ask all the children to sit in a circle, then get them to count to four, clapping their hands at the same time. After each count of four, ask each child their name. Then give them a sticker to put on.

Ring-a-Ring o' Roses
••••

Now you have got each child talking a little bit, it is time to start 'moving' them!

Have the children standing in a circle. They will already be seated in a circle, so all they have to do is stand up and hold hands. Then you, and the circle of children, walk around singing the song. The children will know it even if you don't.

of their own. This way the children won't panic too much as they can still see and hear their parents, and the adults can have a relaxing time too.

Have some nursery rhymes playing in the background (Uncle Mac's *Hello Children Everywhere* is perfect). Guide the children to the colouring station.

Colouring station
••••

All this needs to be is a small coffee table covered with a white paper tablecloth and enough wax crayons for all the children to use. Leave the children here 'settling-in' and creating their masterpieces until everybody has arrived.

Story with actions
••••

This is a great way to 'break the ice' and make the children feel at home. If there are any other adults around get them to join in as well. This will really relax the children, and make things a lot easier for you.

Pick a well-known story. Hunt around for a book with lots of bright colourful pictures as children love to see these (try your local library). Check through the book first

Do s and Don'ts

OOPS! **DON'T** make too much fuss of the children as they arrive since the majority will be feeling rather shy. Thank them for their presents – this will make them feel welcome.

OOPS! **DON'T** let your child open the presents yet, have a little table or somewhere set up ready and keep all the presents together.

The Farmer's in his Den

••••

The children stay standing up in a circle. One of the children becomes the farmer and stands in the middle of the circle (try the birthday child, or a child who is feeling quite confident, it can be a boy or a girl).

The children then move around singing – the child in the middle chooses the wife, the wife then chooses the child and so on…

The Farmer's in his Den,
The Farmer's in his Den,
Eee-aye, Eee-aye,
The Farmer's in his Den.
The Farmer wants a Wife,
The Farmer wants a Wife,
Eee-aye, Eee-aye,
The Farmer wants a Wife.
(A wife is chosen)

The Wife wants a Child,
The Wife wants a Child,
Eee-aye, Eee-aye,
The Wife wants a Child.
(A child is chosen)

The Child wants a Nurse.......
(A nurse is chosen)

The Nurse wants a Dog.......
(A dog is chosen)

We all pat the Dog.......

The Dog wants a Bone.......
(A bone is chosen – everybody then picks the bone while singing)

We all pick the Bone,
We all pick the Bone,
Eee-aye, Eee-aye,
We all pick the Bone.

that. They won't stay still very long but they enjoy rolling around on the floor together.

Teatime
• • • •

Arrange the children into a long line behind the birthday child and tell them they are now the Birthday Train. Get them to hold onto each other around the tummy. Ask them all to make a noise like a train and then lead them off to tea. This makes teatime seem a bit more exciting.

Puppets
• • • •

A puppet show is a good way of stopping the children racing around straight after they've eaten.

If you don't have access to any puppets, then hide behind a sofa or a table and hold up some cuddly toys and sing nursery rhymes with the children. It may sound a bit silly but the children will love it.

Alternatively, you can buy fairly reasonably priced cardboard puppet theatres (*see page 71 for suppliers*).

All the nursery rhymes mentioned already in this chapter would be good for puppets.

Pass the Parcel
• • • •

(See *Party Games* on page 9). With this age group, as the wrappers are removed, ask all the children to join in and sing a favourite nursery rhyme, such as:

☆ Humpty Dumpty
☆ Twinkle, Twinkle, Little Star
☆ Three Blind Mice
☆ The Grand Old Duke of York
☆ Mary, Mary, Quite Contrary
☆ Little Bo Peep

Musical Bumps
• • • •

(See *Party Games* on page 9). You will have to help the children here – ask them to jump up and down, rather than dance (at this age that is how they dance).

Sleeping Lions
• • • •

(See *Party Games* on page 9). Three-year olds will love roaring like lions, so play on

Hokey-cokey
• • • •

This is my version of the Hokey-cokey for little ones.

> You put your fingers in,
> Your fingers out,
> In out, in out,
> You shake them all about.
> You do the Hokey-cokey
> and you turn around.
> That's what it's all about.
>
> Oh! the Hokey-cokey
> Oh! the Hokey-cokey
> Oh! the Hokey-cokey
> Knees bent, arms stretched ra ra ra…

Other verses.....
Ears
Tummies
Big toes
Noses
Your whole self in.

The Wheels on the Bus
• • • •

The wheels on the bus go round and round
(*rotate arms*)
Round and round, round and round
The wheels on the bus go round and round
All day long.

Other verses:
The wipers on the bus go swish, swish, swish
(*move forearms backwards and forwards like windscreen wipers*)

The horn on the bus goes beep, beep, beep
(*mime pressing the horn*)

Here we go round the Mulberry Bush
• • • •

Reform a circle, and move around asking the children to think of things that you do on a cold and frosty morning.

Here we go round the Mulberry Bush,
the Mulberry Bush, the Mulberry Bush.
Here we go round the Mulberry Bush,
On a cold and frosty morning.

This is the way we wash our face,
wash our face, wash our face.
This is the way we wash our face,
On a cold and frosty morning.

Stand-up spot
• • • •

All you do here is make the children sit in a circle and ask if any of them would like to stand up and sing a nursery rhyme.

Lucky Dip
• • • •

Fill a cardboard box with either shredded paper or sawdust and hide party bags or going-home gifts for everyone in amongst the paper or sawdust. Invite each child to dip in as they go home.

Additional Checklist
⤳

Two weeks before the party
• • • •

☆ If your child is going to have a costume, start to prepare it

Three days before the party
• • • •

☆ Buy sawdust or make shredded paper for the lucky dip
☆ Find wax crayons for the colouring station

On the party day
• • • •

☆ Set up the colouring station
☆ Organize the lucky dip

Extras inside your party prop box
• • • •

☆ Music (Uncle Mac's *Hello Children Everywhere* is great for this age)
☆ Wax crayons for the colouring station
☆ White paper tablecloth
☆ One or two story books
☆ Soft toys or puppets

The End of the Party
• • • •

Thank all the children for coming and ask them to give themselves a big clap, then play soft party music as they leave. Make sure that everyone gets a party bag and a balloon if you are giving them as well.

Easy-to-make costumes for fairies and elves

Fairy costume

A pink or white swimming costume or leotard can be used as the base of the costume. All you need is about 2m (6½ft) of net material (available from all department stores).

Fold the net in half and make running stitches with elasticated thread around the folded part of the material, then just add a hook and eye to fasten it around the waist. Put this around the middle of the swimming costume and you have a tutu any three-year-old ballerina would be proud of!

Fairy wand

You need card, a wooden spoon or length of bamboo, sticky tape and silver foil.

Cut out two star shapes from the card and stick them over the bowl of the wooden spoon or on the end of the bamboo with sticky tape. Cover the wand and the stars with silver foil, securing it with tape.

Tiara

You need card, an Alice band, sticky tape and silver foil.

Cut out a triangle from the card big enough to fit onto the Alice band. Secure it with sticky tape and cover with silver foil.

Elf costume

This is really easy to assemble. All you need is a pair of red or green tights to fit the child, an adult's green or red top, a jumper for making a big fat tummy (to be stuffed up the front of the top the child is wearing), a belt to secure the big fat tummy, a woolly hat and a pair of wellington boots.

Decorations

To make a fairy grotto, use lots of pink balloons and streamers, fairy lights; even flowers and branches from the garden. Tableware is readily available for this theme (see page 71 for suppliers).

Mad Hatter's Tea Party

● ● ● ●

This is an easy alternative theme. Send out hat-shaped invitations. Ask the children to wear the hat of their choice; they can wear a funny hat, their favourite hat or they can decorate a hat.

Try to find a hat story to read at the party – even pass the parcel around in a hat! Play *Musical Hats* (see page 42) instead of *Musical Bumps*.

Party tips

★

Party helpers are essential but don't have too many.

★

Two hours is just about long enough for the party, for the children and most certainly for you!

★

Lunch time and early afternoon parties are much better for younger children; late afternoon or early evening parties are best for older children.

★

Do make sure you know exactly what you are doing before the party starts (follow the party plans), and that you are completely clear on the instructions for each game.

Toadstool House

*4-egg Madeira cake mixture (see recipe on
page 21) baked in a 2.3 litre (4 pt) basin
and a 793 g (1³/₄ lb) can
225 g (8 oz) apricot glaze (see page 22)
225 g (8 oz) yellow fondant icing
cornflour for dusting
225 g (8 oz) red fondant icing
125 g (4 oz) green buttercream
liquorice allsorts
chocolate vermicelli
50 g (2 oz) royal icing, coloured brown
cotton wool*

1. Bake the cakes at 170°C (325°F/Gas
Mark 3) for 1¹/₂ hours for the basin and
1¹/₄ hours for the can. Brush both cakes
with apricot glaze and set aside. Roll out
the yellow fondant icing to a 28 cm (11 in)
circle and place over the basin cake.
Smooth it over the top, easing the surplus
icing underneath, using cornflour to prevent it sticking to your hands.

2. Roll out the red fondant icing to an
oblong measuring 36 cm x 10 cm (14 x
4 in). Place round the sides of the cylindri-
cal cake, moulding the join together, and
trim off the excess.

3. Roll out the red trimmings and cut out
circles with a 2.5 cm (1 in) plain cutter.
Stick these onto the yellow cake using a

To make ladybirds
Shape red fondant icing into circular moulds and mark a line down the centre with a knife. Paint black dots and a face using black food colouring.

Madeira Cake
(Double the quantity for an 8-egg mixture)

300 g (10 oz) plain flour
10 ml (2 tsp) baking powder
225 g (8 oz) margarine
225 g (8 oz) caster sugar
grated rind of $^1/2$ a lemon
4 eggs
45 ml (3 tbsp) milk

1. Line and grease the required tin. Sift the flour and baking powder together and set aside. Cream the butter and sugar together in a bowl with the lemon rind until light and fluffy.

2. Beat in the eggs, one at a time, adding 15 ml (1 tbsp) flour with each egg after the first 2 eggs. Carefully fold in the remaining flour, then add the milk. Pour the mixture into the prepared tin and bake at the temperature and time given in the individual recipes, until firm in the centre. Leave the cake in the tin for 5 minutes, then turn out onto a wire rack to cool.

little egg white to attach. Place the yellow cake centrally onto the red base and place on a cake board.

4. Slice the liquorice allsorts to make windows and a door. Pipe on window panes and door handle with the royal icing, then stick them onto the red base. Stick liquorice allsorts on the roof to resemble a chimney, using egg white to attach, and add a little cotton wool to resemble smoke.

5. Spread green buttercream on the cake board and rough up with a palette knife. Sprinkle chocolate vermicelli on the icing to resemble a path leading up to the door.

To make elves
Mould wellington boots and hats from green fondant icing and leave to dry overnight. Mould bodies and arms from red icing, attach a grey belt to each one using egg white and leave to dry. Shape faces from pale pink icing. When they are all dry, assemble using egg white to attach the pieces. Paint eyes and nose using black colouring.

Victoria Sandwich

CAKE QUANTITY	BUTTER OR MARGARINE	CASTER SUGAR	EGGS	SELF-RAISING FLOUR	HOT WATER
3 - egg	175 g (6 oz)	175 g (6 oz)	3	175 g (6 oz)	15 ml (1 tbsp)
4 - egg	225 g (8 oz)	225 g (8 oz)	4	225 g (8 oz)	30 ml (2 tbsp)
5 - egg	300 g (10 oz)	300 g (10 oz)	5	300 g (10 oz)	45 ml (3 tbsp)
6 - egg	350 g (12 oz)	350 g (12 oz)	6	350 g (12 oz)	45 ml (3 tbsp)

1. Line and grease the required tin. Cream the butter and sugar in a bowl until light and fluffy. Beat in the eggs, one at a time, adding 15 ml (1 tbsp) flour with each egg after the first one. Fold in the remaining flour with a metal spoon, then add the hot water.

2. Pour the mixture into the prepared tin and bake at the temperature and time given in the individual recipes, until the cake springs back when lightly pressed. Turn onto a wire rack to cool.

To colour coconut
● ● ● ●

Place the desiccated coconut in a small bowl. Mix a few drops of food colouring and water together and stir into the coconut with a spoon, until evenly coloured.

Apricot glaze
● ● ● ●

Place 450 g (1 lb) apricot jam in a saucepan with 60 ml (4 tbsp) water and heat gently until dissolved. Sieve and return to the pan, reheating before use. This will keep in the refrigerator for several months.

To colour fondant icing
● ● ● ●

Add a few drops of food colouring to white fondant icing and knead well together using rubber gloves to prevent staining your hands.

Knead thoroughly until there are no streaks left.

4–5 year olds
Peter Pan and Pirates

At-a-Glance Party Plan

Decorating Treasure Island place mats

Name Game

Musical Bumps

Islands

Shipwreck

Pass the Treasure Box (box version of Pass the Parcel)

Sleeping Peters (a variation of Sleeping Lions)

Teatime

Stand-up spot

Puppet show — Peter Pan story

Grandmother's Footsteps

Treasure Hunt

Hokey-cokey

This age group are by now getting used to the party scene. They generally love parties, but they can still be a bit shy. As long as you start off gently they will soon get into the swing of things. They are usually very excited and extremely agreeable.

If some parents are staying to help, that's great. If they are not going to be involved, try to persuade them to leave quickly. It really tips the balance with this age if some children have their parents hanging around and others don't.

Peter Pan is a good theme for children of this age. It's a great story with lots of fun characters, giving you plenty to work with.

Invitations
• • • •

In keeping with the Peter Pan theme, you can make invitations in the shape of Treasure Islands. These are very easy to do. All you need is plenty of yellow card, crayons or colouring pencils and scissors. Cut out island-shaped invitations. Trace around the islands with a blue crayon to

represent sea. Then draw palm trees, treasure chests, crocodiles, quicksand…your child will enjoy helping you!

Decorating Treasure Island place mats
• • • •

These are a larger version of the Treasure Island invitations, but this time just cut out the island shapes and leave them for the children to decorate. You will need a covered table for them to work on, glue, and something to use as decoration – magazines, tissue paper, felt pens or crayons. This will occupy the children while the other guests are arriving.

Name Game
• • • •

(See *Party Games* on page 9). The birthday child should start by telling everyone their name and, if they are in fancy dress, who they are dressed up to be, how old they are and what their favourite colour is. Then start the clapping again and move around to the next person.

Musical Bumps
• • • •

(See *Party Games* on page 9).

Islands
• • • •

Give everyone a postcard-sized or slightly bigger piece of paper, (this is their island). Ask them to find a space and stand on their island. Play music and ask the children to walk or skip around the room, then as the music stops they must stand on the nearest island to them – only one person per island. They must not stand on the same one each turn. Remove one or two islands each round. Anyone who doesn't have an island becomes a judge.

Party tips

★

Decorate the house with balloons and give one to everyone to take home. That way you won't be left with dozens of deflating balloons for weeks on end.

★

Do keep pets out of the way. Some children will be very scared of them, and vice versa!

★

Don't have the entertainment area near a main door or anywhere else where there will be distractions.

★

Set up a separate area for adults away from the main entertainment area.

Shipwreck
• • • •

All you do here is call out commands and the children follow. The last person to follow a command becomes a judge. This can be great fun but don't let it go on for too long, as the children get tired. The commands are:

Climb the rigging: ask children to run on the spot, using their arms to pretend to climb up the rigging.

Captain's coming: the children call out *Aye Aye Captain* and salute.

Scrub the deck: the children mime scrubbing the deck.

Starboard: the children have to rush to one side of the room.

Portside: the children have to rush to the other side of the room.

Man overboard: the children all lie on the floor pretending to float.

Pass the Treasure Box
● ● ● ●

This is very similar to Pass the Parcel (see *Party Games* on page 9 for the rules of Pass the Parcel). All you do here is put the prize into different-sized boxes, getting smaller and smaller – so each time the children have to open boxes, instead of unwrapping paper. Inside each box, put the title of a song for the children to sing.

The following are good songs to choose:
☆ Happy Birthday
☆ Twinkle, Twinkle, Little Star
☆ If you're Happy and you know it
☆ Ten green bottles
or ask your child if there are some special songs the children sing at school.

Sleeping Peters
••••

This is a variation of *Sleeping Lions*, on page 10. Instead of lions, get the children to fly around the room like Peter Pan.

Teatime
••••

You can use the Birthday Train idea here (see page 16), but get everybody to fly.

Stand-up spot
••••

Ask if any of the children would like to stand up and tell a joke or sing a song. If everyone wants to and they all start to rush at you, say that you will choose someone who is sitting down. They will all quickly sit down!

Puppet Show
••••

You can buy very reasonably priced cardboard puppet theatres (*see page 71 for suppliers*) or you can hide behind the furniture. Try to have a go at a very simple Peter Pan story (you can always get the book from your local library). If you feel you can't, ask the children to have a go. Put them into groups of twos or threes, give them a couple of puppets or soft toys and ask them to think of a nursery rhyme (using the puppets) to show to everyone. Pop around to each group and give them a bit of help.

Grandmother's Footsteps
••••

Ask someone to be the Grandmother (maybe choose the birthday child). They must stand at one end of the room facing the wall. All the other children line up at the opposite end of the room and creep silently towards the Grandmother. As soon as she hears a sound, she must turn around and send anyone who is moving back to the beginning again. When someone touches Grandmother, they change places and start again.

Treasure Hunt

• • • •

Using gold coins, cheap jewellery and lots of paper clues, the children have to all work together to find the going-home bags. You can put the children into groups and give a little prize for the group that makes the discovery. If you are having a summertime party and have a garden, this is ideal. If not, restrict it to the house but make sure you don't hide the clues in the leaves of expensive plants or behind priceless ornaments!

Hokey-cokey

• • • •

(See page 17). Ask the children what parts of the body they would like to put in each time.

Additional Checklist

☆ A large island shape for each child to decorate, plus decorating materials – glue, old magazines, tissue paper, colouring pencils
☆ Paper or card to make the islands for the Islands game
☆ Boxed *Pass the Parcel*
☆ Puppet show and puppets or soft toys
☆ Items for treasure hunt – clues, jewellery, coins etc

Easy-to-make ideas for the Peter Pan theme

Peter Pan is a great theme which lends itself to a wealth of games and ideas. The children can dress up as the following:

Peter Pan
Wendy
The rest of the Darling children
Captain Hook and pirates
Tinkerbell

Costumes
• • • •

The costumes are very simple:

Peter Pan: all Peter really needs is a green leotard and tights, with a waistcoat over the top.

Wendy: just a nightie

Captain Hook and pirates: stripey T-shirt, black eye patch, neckerchief or bandana tied around the neck or head, a painted-on moustache.

Tinkerbell: a fairy costume (see fairy costume ideas on page 19).

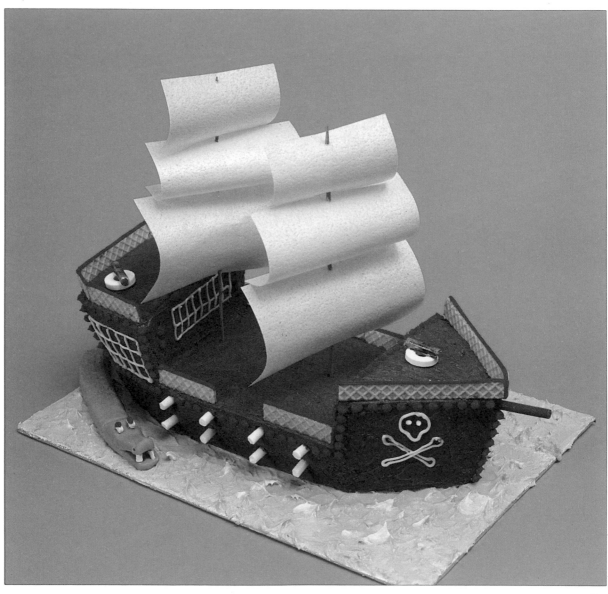

Pirate Galleon Cake

3-egg Victoria sandwich cake mixture (see
  chart on page 22) baked in a 20 x 30 cm
  (8 x 12 in) Swiss roll tin
chocolate buttercream
1 packet wafers
1 chocolate candy stick
candy sticks
mint sweets
175 g (6 oz) royal icing, 125 g (4 oz) of it
  coloured red
rice paper
2 long satay sticks or straws
50 g (2 oz) blue buttercream

1. Bake the cake at 180°C (350°F/Gas Mark 4) for 30 minutes. Cut the cake across into 3 equal portions, stick 2 together with chocolate buttercream. Place on a cakeboard.

2. Cut the remaining slice across into 3 equal pieces.Cut one piece in half again.

3. Stick the 2 smallest oblongs together and place behind the large cake. Stick the 2 remaining oblongs together and place on top, as shown.

Cut off the bow end to a point giving 4 triangular pieces.

4. Invert these pieces and place on the bow, sticking them together with chocolate butter cream.

5. Slice off the back of the cake at an angle to form the stern and cut off a slight angle at the side.

6. Cover the whole cake with chocolate buttercream, smooth evenly with a palette knife and place on a board.

7. Cut the wafers into 4 lengthways and stand upright all round the edges of the decks, and put a chocolate candy stick in to make a bowsprit.

8. Cut candy sticks into short lengths and push into the side of the cake to represent guns. Place a mint sweet with a candy stick on top of it on the bow and at each corner of the stern to represent cannons.

9. Pipe windows and a skull and crossbones, using white royal icing. Decorate around the wafers, and where desired, with red royal icing, using a piping bag fitted with a small fluted nozzle.

10. Cut rice paper into oblongs of graduating size and thread onto the satay sticks to represent sails. Cover the cake board with blue buttercream and mark into waves with a palette knife. Mould a crocodile from green fondant icing, if desired, leaving it to set overnight.

SAFETY HINTS

After tea, do make sure that you have a slightly damp cloth around to wipe sticky fingers, this will save your furniture and walls.

Do be careful about giving young children any type of nuts or large boiled sweets.

5–6 year olds
Animal Crackers!

At-a-Glance Party Plan

Name Game

Musical Statues

Pass the Parcel with forfeits

Emus and Elephants

What's the Time, Mr Wolf

Sleeping Lions

Teatime

Face Painting

Pin the Tail on the Donkey

Flap the Fish

Cats and Dogs

Chinese Whispers

Animals are the theme of this chapter. Children of this age are by now fairly sociable and firm partygoers! They will most certainly be fascinated by animals and will love imitating the sounds and movements they make. They love to have their faces painted, and animals are amongst the easiest to tackle. Sometimes a few children might refuse to join in. Try not to let anyone drop out as this can be terribly infectious, just make sure that you have plenty of ideas up your sleeve and everything will be fine.

Invitations
....

Plain white postcards are ideal. Give your child a stack of magazines, glue, rounded-ended scissors and colouring pencils. Ask him/her to find as many animal pictures as possible and stick these on the front of the card. They could also draw their own scene for the animal – jungle, desert, garden – whatever is appropriate.

If you are going to try your luck at a bit of face painting make sure that you forewarn the parents on the invitation, in case they have plans to take the children out after the party! Also, you may discover a child has an allergy or skin disorder, so it is always polite to check. Make sure you buy the right type of water-based face paints (*see page 71 for suppliers*) as these are all allergy-tested and will not harm the children's skin (as well as being very easy to use).

Name Game
• • • •

(See *Party Games* on page 9). Ask the children not only to tell their name, but also their favourite animal and anything they know about it. Can they make a noise like their animal?

Musical Statues
• • • •

(See *Party Games* on page 9). If you are going to follow through the animal theme, change the name to Musical Animals. Tell the children that while the music is playing they should dance as their animal would move. Even if you are not following the theme of animals, it works very well with this age group to give them a command each time the music stops. Ask them to freeze (stand still), then call out a command (e.g Tiger). The children have to then think about how a tiger stands, find the position and freeze. You can do this with any type of statue e.g ballerina, astronaut. It

helps the children to think a bit more about what they are doing rather than just playing a game and they also get much more fun out of it. Don't forget to praise them, because they will try really hard – a little 'Well Done' is enough to make them feel really good and of course, they will then try even harder.

Pass the Parcel
• • • •

(See *Party Games* on page 9). This is played in the usual way, except between each layer you place a forfeit. This adds a great deal of fun and excitement to the game. The forfeits could be animal-related:

☆ Hop around the room like a kangaroo
☆ Swim like a fish
☆ Oink like a pig
or they could be something like these:
☆ Sing a song
☆ Tell a joke

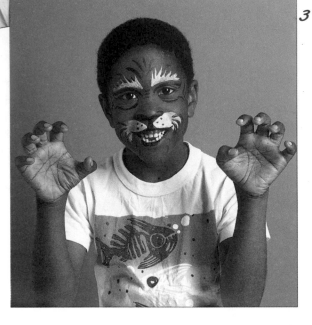

☆ Kiss the person next to you (great for mixed parties – this will make everybody scream!)

Emus and Elephants
• • • •

This is a good quick game for waking everybody up. Every time you call out 'Elephants' the children have to run to one end of the room, pretending to be an elephant with a trunk waving around (children use their arm as a trunk). Every time you call out 'Emus', the children have to run to the other end of the room with their arm up in the air pretending to be an emu (their arm representing the emu's long neck). The last person to reach the end has to be a judge. You should be left with just one child – the winner.

What's the Time, Mr Wolf?
• • • •

Ask someone (usually the birthday child) to be Mr Wolf. The child then walks around the room and the rest of the children follow. They all ask 'What's the time, Mr Wolf?' repeatedly. The wolf calls out various times. Nothing happens until the wolf calls out 'Lunchtime' and then the children have to run to home and safety. I usually make a clear wall home, where not too much can get broken. If the wolf manages to catch one of the children before they reach home, they become the new wolf.

Sleeping Lions
• • • •

(See *Party Games* on page 9).

Teatime

• • • •

Get them all into a train and tell them they
are heading off for the chimps' tea party.

Face Painting

• • • •

Here are a few ideas for you to follow. If
you have a large number of children, make
sure that there is someone around to help
you otherwise they will get bored waiting
for their turn and all hell will break loose!
If you have a small number of children and
there is just you, you can always ask them
to help by giving you suggestions. Ask
them what colours to use for certain animals – what does a tiger's nose look like?

Do s and Don'ts

YAH! **DO** keep the decorations simple
and to a minimum (as the children will pull them down given
the chance). This will save you
time, and calm your nerves.

YAH! **DO** warn parents if you are going
to do face painting; they may be
planning to take the children out
after the party.

YAH! **DO** have someone to help with
face painting, otherwise the children will get bored while they
wait for their turn.

OOPS! **DON'T** let anyone drop out of
activities like face painting; it can
be terribly infectious. Just make
sure you have plenty of ideas up
your sleeve and everything will
be fine.

Pin the Tail on the Donkey
• • • •

This can be played while the rest of the children are having their faces painted. You can buy this game from most party shops (*see page 71 for suppliers*) already made up, or you can make your own. All you have to do is to draw a large picture of a donkey without a tail – you will need a separate tail. Mark with a cross where the tail should be. Each child is blindfolded in turn and given the tail. They are then turned around three times and guided towards the donkey picture. The child then has to pin the tail on the donkey. The nearest person to the cross wins.

Flap the Fish
• • • •

(See *Party Games* on page 9).

Cats and Dogs
• • • •

Everyone forms a circle. One child stands in the middle of the circle, that child is the

Additional Checklist
⊆

Three weeks before the party
• • •

☆ Buy or make animal invitations
☆ Buy animal tableware
☆ Buy face paints (start practising)
☆ Make your child's ears and tail, if wearing

One week before the party
• • •

☆ Check if you have the music, tableware, face paints
☆ Make sure you have a donkey picture for Pin the Tail on the Donkey game

Extras inside your party prop box
• • •

☆ Music tapes, such as *Nellie the Elephant*, *Birdy song*
☆ Cut-out of two fish and two bundles of newspaper for Flap the Fish game.
☆ Pass the Parcel and forfeits
☆ Donkey and donkey tail
☆ Pen

cat. All the other children are dogs. When the cat is ready it walks around the outside of the circle. With a very loud meow, the cat touches the back of one of the dogs and starts to run around the circle in a clockwise direction. The dog must chase the cat by running in the same direction only. The first person to get back to the dog's original place becomes a dog, the other is the cat. So if the dog fails to reach the cat, he/she then becomes the cat. This is quite a fast game; make sure there are no breakable objects about. If things start to get out of hand, ask the children to walk.

Chinese Whispers
• • • •

(See *Party Games* on page 9).

Theme Costumes
• • • •

With an animal theme, and the fact that you're going to be doing some face painting, the children really don't need to turn up in fancy dress. But if you want to go for it, then why not? Alternatively, just ask the children to wear a pair of ears and a tail of the animal of their choice.

Safety tip for Face painting
• • • •

If any of the children have an open wound, cold sore or any skin complaint, avoid that area. You will be suprised how contagious such things are, and you don't want to be responsible for any major outbreaks amongst your child's friends! If you do happen to paint over anything like this, don't use the brush or the sponge on anyone else. If a child has a very bad skin problem, you can always paint their hand or arm.

Elephant Cake

5-egg Victoria sandwich cake mixture (see chart on page 22) baked in two 20 cm (8 in) sandwich tins
450 g (1 lb) grey fondant icing
25 g (1 oz) white fondant icing
125 g (4 oz) green buttercream
225 g (8 oz) apricot glaze (see page 22)
cornflour for dusting
egg white
2 pink sugar balls
4 pink sugar-coated chocolate sweets

1. Bake the cakes at 180°C (350°F/Gas Mark 4) for 40-45 minutes. Roll out a little of the grey fondant icing and cut out 2 ears (see photograph). Allow them to set resting on a plate to give the ear shape. Make a tail from grey icing and leave overnight. Make tusks from white icing and leave to set.

2. Cut the bottom quarter off each cake. Sandwich the cake together with some of the buttercream and cut an arc, as shown.

3. Cut out the shaded area and set aside for

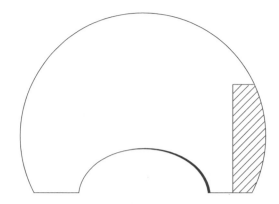

the trunk. Shape off the rounded edges. Trim the cake away at an angle to form the face. Brush with apricot glaze all over.

4. Roll out the remaining grey fondant icing to a 35 cm (14 in) circle. Lay it over the elephant and mould to shape. Reserve the trimmings.

5. To make the trunk, shape the cut off piece of cake to form a trunk; the top is wide narrowing down to the end of the trunk. Cover with apricot glaze and then with grey fondant icing. Place in position on the board and carefully mould to the main body, using cornflour on your fingers. Alternatively, make a trunk from fondant icing; leaving to dry overnight before positioning.

6. Attach the ears, tusks and tail with egg white. Stick on the pink sugar balls for eyes and attach the sugar-coated chocolate sweets to the feet. Spread the remaining green buttercream over the cake board to resemble grass.

SAFETY HINTS

✖

Are there any heavy objects that could possibly fall? Do make sure that heavy free-standing bookcases are secure, iron candlesticks are pushed far back onto shelves or removed altogether, and remember, if you have several children dancing, certain objects in the room will move or vibrate, however solid they may appear. Have a really good safety check before you start.

✖

If you are booking a venue, do check around and make sure everything looks safe. Check the catches on the outside and loo doors. If the hall is close to a main road, then make sure that you keep the door closed at all times. Check there are adequate facilites and that everything is reasonably clean. A telephone nearby is a must.

✖

If you decide to do face painting, do use allergy-free paints (*see page 71 for suppliers*). Make sure that they are specifically for face painting, as ordinary artists' paints will damage children's skin.

6-7 year olds
Team Game Fun

At-a-Glance Party Plan

Name Game

Guess the Sound

Team Games
Ladders
Flap the Fish
Pass the Balloon
Nosey Parker
Thread the Team
Human Noughts and Crosses
Memory Tray

Smell the Smell

Pinata

Teatime

Musical Hats

Musical Stands

Bubblegum

This age group are great fun at parties. They usually have a full entertainment calendar and are very used to the party scene and all manner of social activities. Also, as they have been going to school for a while, they know how to behave. They will have a firm idea of who they want to invite and will look forward to the party for weeks and weeks! Now is a really good time for you and your child to plan and work together on a party. They will really enjoy helping and they will give you plenty of ideas and advice!

A good, easy theme to follow for the six-to-seven year olds is a colour theme. You can either choose one colour, for example a red party, or you can ask everyone to turn up in their favourite colour, and have a real mish-mash of colour everywhere. Alternatively, given the fact that the party plan contains a lot of team games, you can ask half the children to turn up in one

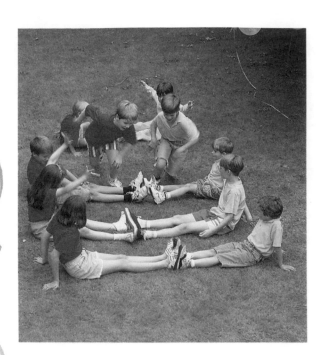

colour and the other half another colour, so you might have a red team and a blue team!

Invitations
• • • •

If you have decided on a one-colour party, you can buy postcards in that colour for your invitations or you can use white postcards and get your child to colour them.

Name Game
• • • •

(See *Party Games* on page 9). Ask the children to tell everyone their name and a little bit about themselves, such as what their favourite colour is, what they like to do, have they got brothers and sisters.

Guess the Sound
• • • •

This is a great focusing type of game. All you need to do is to play a tape of sound effects (you can buy these or you can make your own) and the children have to try to guess what the sound is. Make a note of who has guessed what and the person who guesses the most is the winner.

Team Games
• • • •

Put the children into two teams. The next few games are all played in these two teams.

Ladders: The teams sit opposite each other with their legs extended and feet touching. They should be in two lines. Give each pair of children a number. All you have to do is call out any number at random. On hearing their number the pair must stand up and run down the leg ladder, back up the outside and back down the leg ladder to their places. The first one back to their place wins their team a point.

Flap the Fish: The children stay in their teams. (See *Party Games* on page 9).

Pass the Balloon: Each team is now given a balloon. They must pass the balloon down the line by putting the balloon between their legs. The no-touch rule applies. Once the balloon reaches the end of the line, it then has to be passed back up the line under the chin. Again the no-touch rule applies. The first team to return the balloon to the front of the line is the winner.

Nosey Parker: Still in their teams, the children stay standing behind each other. Each team is given a matchbox sleeve. The only way the matchbox sleeve can be passed is by the nose. The children are not allowed to touch the

Dos and Don'ts

OOPS! DON'T leave loose balloons around the party room as fights and mayhem will break out (everyone will want one, probably the same one).

YAH! DO make sure the games aren't too long. As soon as the children show signs of getting bored, move on.

YAH! DO make sure you have a contingency plan in case it rains, if you are having the party in the garden!

matchboxes except with their noses. If anyone is caught cheating that team has to start again. The first team to pass the matchbox all the way down the line and back again are the winners.

Thread the Team: A long piece of string with a weighty object such as a key on it, is given to each team. They have to thread the string through everybody's shirts and the first team to string everybody together is the winner.

Human Noughts and Crosses: One team becomes the noughts, the others become the crosses. Nine markers, such as cushions or cards, mark out a large noughts and crosses board. All you do is literally play human noughts and crosses.

Memory Tray: A tray full of objects is brought out. The tray is shown to both

Additional Checklist

☆ Sound effects tape

☆ Paper and pen

☆ Fish (for flapping)

☆ Newspaper to flap the fish

☆ Two matchbox sleeves

☆ Balloons

☆ Two keys on strings

☆ Noughts and crosses markers

☆ Memory tray and objects for it

☆ Hats for Musical Hats

☆ Objects to smell, such as a spoonful
   of jam, perfume, washing powder,
   cheese, old training shoe, flower

☆ Papier-mâché model (Pinata)

☆ Sweets and goodies to fill the Pinata

teams at the same time for 1 minute, then taken away. Whilst the tray is out nobody is allowed to talk. As soon as the tray has left the room each team is given a paper and pencil. They then have 1 minute to remember everything that was on the tray. The team that remembers the most is the winner.

Smell the Smell
• • • •

Everyone gets into a long line. In turn, everyone is blindfolded as they reach the head of the queue. While there, they are given something to smell. They must try to identify it.

Pinata
• • • •

A papier-mâché model (*see step-by-step guide*) is filled with sweets and hung up out of the children's reach. One by one, each child is given the chance to swipe (with a stick or a broom handle) three times at the model, until it bursts open.

Equipment: *one large balloon, plenty of newspaper, flour and water paste, heavy twine, tissue paper, crepe paper, sweets and small gifts.*

1. Blow up the balloon and tie (this forms the body of the pinata). Mix the flour and water to a smooth paste. Tear newspaper into strips, dip into the paste and lay the strips across the balloon.

2. Wrap twine twice around. Tie at the top, leaving enough twine to hang the pinata. Continue to cover the balloon. Hang to dry for about 4 days.

3. Cut a circular hole near the twine. Remove the section and fill with small gifts and sweets. Reposition section. Decorate the pinata using tissue and crepe papers. Animals and birds are popular.

The sweets cascade out everywhere! Have a bowl to hand, so that all the findings can be put into the bowl and shared out into the going-home bags.

Teatime
• • • •

Lead all the colours to the tea table in their team groups.

Musical Hats
• • • •

A big pile of hats is put into the centre of the room. As the music plays, everyone has to dance or jump around the hats. As soon as the music stops, all the players have to rush and grab one. Give the children a couple of practices with a hat for everyone. As soon as they have got the hang of it, start to take the hats away. Make sure that nobody cheats.

Musical Stands
• • • •

Very similar to *Musical Bumps* (See *Party Games* on page 9), except when the music plays the players sit down and dance on their bottoms, and when the music stops they stand up!

Bubblegum
• • • •

(See *Party Games* on page 9).

Swimming pool cake (opposite)

Swimming Pool Cake

6-egg Victoria sandwich cake mixture (see
   chart on page 22) baked in two 23 cm
   (9 in) sandwich tins
225 g (8 oz) chocolate buttercream
45 ml (3 tbsp) apricot glaze (see page 22)
125 g (4 oz) fondant icing (coloured 2 shades
   of blue)
cornflour for dusting
1 packet chocolate mint crisps
chocolate vermicelli
125 g (4 oz) green buttercream
desiccated coconut, coloured green (see page 22)
candy sticks
sugar-coated chocolate sweets
1 packet wafers
liquorice allsorts
mint sweets
red food colouring

SAFETY HINTS

✖

Are there any sharp surfaces such as
edges of shelves or tables? If things do
get out of control, and the children start
to run around, is there anything that
they could bump into and cut or injure
themselves on?

✖

If the party is in the garden, are there
any areas that you should rope off
(compost heaps, ditches, water, unsafe
walls, bramble bushes)?

✖

If the party is going to be outside, do
make sure the children are well
protected from the sun. Have enough
sunscreen for everyone and keep
monitoring the children to make sure
nobody gets burnt.

---

1. Bake the cakes at 180°C (350°F/Gas mark 4) for 45-50 minutes. Cut out the swimming pool shape from the top of one of the cakes, as shown in the photograph.

2. Sandwich the cakes together with some of the chocolate buttercream, leaving the area at the base of the cake clear. Place the cake on a cake board.

3. Cut out 3 circular steps from the top cake, starting 4 cm (1½ in) in from the side.

4. Place the discarded piece from these steps at the base of the steps on the board to make the fourth step.

5. Brush glaze over the base and sides of the pool. Roll out the blue fondant icing and use to line the pool. Ease it in carefully, dusting with cornflour to prevent it sticking. Trim off the excess.

6. Cut the mint crisps with a sharp knife to make paving slabs to fit round the pool edge. Ice the sides of the cake and the steps with the remaining chocolate buttercream and coat the sides with chocolate vermicelli. Cut mint crisps to make paving slabs to fit on top of each step.

7. Coat the top of the cake and the board with green buttercream and sprinkle with the coloured coconut. Place two candy sticks into the cake at the top of the steps and attach sugar-coated chocolate sweets with a little icing to represent lamps.

8. Cut the wafers into small squares and stand them upright round part of the top of the cake as a fence.

9. Cut thin slices from liquorice allsorts to make airbeds to float in the pool. Paint the mint sweets with red food colouring to make lifebelts and stick onto the wafers with a little icing.

7-8 year olds
Disco Dancing

At-a-Glance Party Plan

Mask Making

Name Game

Disco Musical Statues

Agadoo

Dancing Competition

Disco Mats

Knots and Tangles

The Locomotion

Teatime

What's my Line?

Am I...?

Chinese Whispers

Disco Groups

Limbo Competition

This can sometimes be a tricky age group! They have seen a lot of parties by this time, and are getting a bit tired of the same old routine. They don't like being ordered about too much and the boys have usually discovered fighting in a big way! However, as long as you establish your authority straight away you should be fine. Children of this age can be fun – very witty and full of spirit. A disco theme is a great idea, but, you must get the music right.

Having decided on the disco theme, it is a good idea to have a mask-making activity for when the children arrive.

It is not really necessary to ask the children to wear fancy dress if you are going to make masks (a great relief to their parents!) However, it might be fun for the children to arrive in a disco style, leaving the choice up to them. They may decide to wear their best party clothes, or they could turn up in some 'glittery number' on loan from a glamorous parent.

Invitations
● ● ● ●

If you are going to follow on with the disco and mask theme, it is quite a good idea to send out invitations to the masked ball. They could be very formal on gold-edged card (available from most card shops), or you can decorate postcards with circles of brightly coloured foil paper (representing disco lights). Cut different-sized circles and stick them to the front of the cards. Your child can do this.

Try to tape lots of current lively music or buy compilation tapes of disco hits. To

create a disco scene, draw the curtains and change the light bulbs to coloured ones. You can hire small columns of lights, disco rigs and bubble machines quite cheaply, if wished (*see page 71 for suppliers*).

Mask Making

● ● ● ●

Have a small table set up with glue, brightly coloured paper, things to stick on such as sequins, foil, tissue paper and glitter and enough basic masks for everyone. These can be bought and then decorated, or made from paper plates, (*see page 71 for mask suppliers*). As they arrive, ask everyone to make their own mask for the masked ball!

Name Game

• • • •

(See *Party Games* on page 9). The children not only tell their name, they also state their favourite colour, music and football team. Decide beforehand what you would like the children to tell you and then ask those questions. Remember that some children will talk the hind leg off a donkey whereas others will not want to utter a word. So try to keep things moving.

Disco Musical Statues

• • • •

(See *Party Games* on page 9 for general rules.) The only difference is the children disco dance while the music is playing. When the music stops, ask them to stand and freeze as a current pop star. Make sure they are people the children know. I suggest that you and your child make a list before you start.

Agadoo

• • • •

(See *Party Games* on page 9).

Dancing Competition

• • • •

Play one tune and ask the children to dance. I think it is a good idea to pick the best girl dancer and the best boy dancer. (I personally don't think you should actually pick the best dancers but the children you can see who are trying the hardest or the children who haven't won anything!)

Disco Mats

• • • •

This is a bit like *Islands* (see *Party Games* on page 9). The only difference is that the children dance around the mats, which can be folded newspaper or cushions.

Knots and Tangles
• • • •

The children dance around the room as the music plays. When the music stops you call out commands such as 'Knee to elbow!' The children then have to find a partner and put their knee to the other person's elbow. This game is great fun and the children always love it. You must tell them to find a new partner each time (to keep everybody mixing with each other), and if there is an odd number of children get them to work in groups of three to make sure that nobody is left out.

Suggested commands:
- ☆ Big toe to nose
- ☆ Head to head
- ☆ Back to back
- ☆ Tummy to little finger

The Locomotion
• • • •

Ask the children to stand in a line behind the birthday child, holding onto the person in front by the shoulders. The music is then put on and the birthday child leads the way. Whatever the leader does the rest of the children have to follow.

Teatime
• • • •

Use *The Locomotion* to dance the children in to tea.

What's my Line?
• • • •

Prepare a selection of cards with various occupations written on them, e.g Gardener, Ballet dancer, Jockey, Secretary, Astronaut, Policeman. Then ask the birthday child to select a card. The other children sit in a circle while the child acts out what is written on the card. He/she is not allowed to speak or to give any clues. The others must guess the occupation. The person who guesses correctly then selects a card and so on.

Am I . . . ?
• • • •

Everyone stays in the circle and a piece of paper is either stuck or pinned to each child's back. Written on the paper is the name of a famous person, fact or fiction. The children have to try and guess who they are by asking each other questions, but the answers can only be 'Yes' or 'No'.

Do s and Don'ts

YAH! DO make sure that you are full of beans before the start of the party. Children will pick up on any feelings of lethargy, fear and anger and will then play on them.

OOPS! DON'T put party blowers on the teatable, they will drive you mad. If your child insists on them, put them in the going-home bags.

OOPS! DON'T put the savoury and sweet things out together, otherwise you will be left with mountains of sandwiches.

Additional Checklist

☆ Mask-making equipment – masks, glue, sticky tape, items to decorate the masks (sequins, foil, tissue paper, glitter)

☆ Disco gear – you can use your usual stereo or cassette player or you can hire a small disco rig at a reasonable cost. Try the *Yellow Pages* or see page 71 for suppliers.

☆ For fun lighting you can have coloured light bulbs or disco lights (again these can be hired – *Yellow Pages* or page 71). Don't forget to draw the curtains to set the disco scene!

☆ Mats – for Disco Mats game. You can use folded newspapers or cushions.

☆ Cards with names of occupations written on them for What's my Line? (make sure you use occupations that the children will know). Sticky labels with famous names written on (enough for everyone) Broomstick and two chairs for Limbo Competition.

Suggested famous people:
☆ Father Christmas
☆ The Queen
☆ Mickey Mouse
☆ Michael Jackson
☆ Maybe, if the children are in the same class, their teacher

Suggested questions:
☆ Am I alive now?
☆ Am I a man or a woman?
☆ Am I on television?

Chinese Whispers
• • • •
(See *Party Games* on page 9).

Disco Groups
• • • •

Back on with the disco music. The children dance around while the music is playing. The music suddenly stops and a number is called out, for instance 'three'. The children must then get themselves into groups of three. Again the music plays, the children dance, then as another number is called they must re-group.

Limbo Competition
• • • •

Place a broomstick on two chairs and arrange the children in a line. One-by-one they must pass under the stick without using their hands. You can make the stick lower and lower, if there is time. But the point of the competition is that everyone is a winner. They all win their going-home bags.

SAFETY HINTS
✖

Do make sure that there are no chemicals or tablets around the house or garden that could be harmful to the children.

✖

Do be careful about heating. If you are having an open fire, make sure it is well guarded (the same for gas and electric bar heaters). Party clothes are very flimsy and could easily go up in flames.

✖

If your party is near water (beach, swimming pool, river) do make sure that you have plenty of strong adult swimmers helping you. Water is great fun but highly dangerous, not having enough adult help could prove fatal!

Disco Cake

*8-egg Madeira cake mixture (see recipe on
   page 21) baked in a 20 x 30 cm (8 x 12 in)
   deep oblong tin*
225 g (8 oz) apricot glaze (see page 22)
750 g (1 ½ lb) fondant icing
blue and red food colourings
1 packet wafers
175 g (6 oz) royal icing, coloured red
silver balls
sugar-coated chocolate sweets
2 liquorice Catherine wheels
liquorice allsorts

1. Bake the cake at 150°C (300°F/Gas Mark 2) for 2 hours. Cut the cake into two 7.5 cm (3 in) pieces, leaving one 15 cm (6 in) wide piece.

2. Cut off the top 4 cm (1½ in) of the large cake, and discard. Cut the bases off each cake so that they stand level and brush all over with apricot glaze.

3. Colour 450 g (1 lb) fondant icing a purple colour and the remainder red. Roll out three-quarters of the purple icing and use to cover the larger piece of cake, moulding the edges together with a palette knife.

4. Add the trimmings to the remaining purple icing and roll out to an oblong measuring 20 x 15 cm (8 x 6 in). Roll the red icing into a similar oblong shape.

5. Cut the oblongs in a zigzag pattern, and arrange them in alternate colours along the sides of the two smaller cakes. Cover the tops of each with purple icing and mould the seams together with a palette knife.

6. Cut 4 cm (1½ in) circles from the wafers using a pastry cutter and stick them onto the 'sound boxes' with a little royal icing. Pipe red royal icing around each one and arrange silver balls on top.

7. Stick sugar-coated chocolate sweets down the sides of the 'sound desk' and pipe rosettes of royal icing along the top and bottom edges. Stick silver balls on top of the rosettes.

8. Place two liquorice Catherine wheels on top of the 'sound desk'. Cut two slices of liquorice allsorts for knobs. Arrange thin slices of wafer over the liquorice for the deck arm.

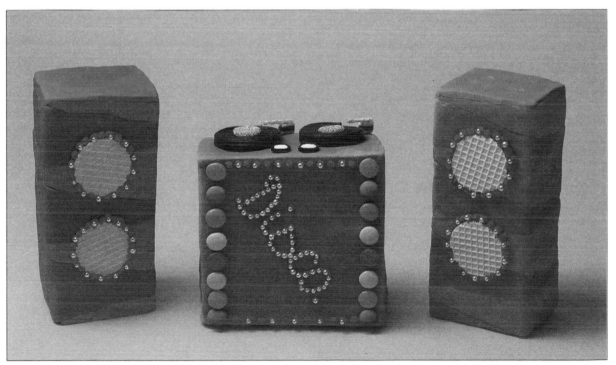

Over 8s Drama Time

At-a-Glance Party Plan

Name Game set to rhythm

Changing Object

Bubblegum

Anagrams

Give Me that Chair!

1-2-3

Chinese Whispers

Spot the Ad

Teatime

Set the Scene

Magic Bowl

Pass the Story

The 'over eights' crowd are a very grown-up bunch and they hate being treated like babies, but do still like to have fun. Handled the right way, they will be game for anything. Drama-based games are ideal for this age group, as they will be yearning for something a little bit different.

I think the main aim here is not to make things too schoolish. Let the children use their own imaginations and have as much fun as possible. They are very responsible at this age so there shouldn't be too much trouble.

Have everything fully prepared. Establish your authority without becoming an 'old tyrant'! The more relaxed and enthusiastic you are, the more the children will join in and have a good time. It really is up to you and your child to set the scene. Let the children take as much responsibilty as possible. They will be more than willing to pass the food around, take coats etc, so do delegate. But, they will need guiding and organizing – don't just leave them to it.

There are several really good themes for this age group. Again, they will be more than happy to dress up if the idea is sold in the right way.

Changing Object
• • • •

Stay in the circle. Place an object (chair, balloon, shoe) in the middle. One-by-one, the children must go into the middle and change the object into something else, through mime and plenty of imagination. I have seen children change a school ruler into a motorbike, toothbrush, chair!

Bubblegum
• • • •

(See *Party Games* on page 9).

Anagrams
• • • •

Take about ten sheets and write, in large lettering, one jumbled word on each sheet. Make the first couple quite easy and then get gradually harder. Try the following suggestions: school, homework, football, sausages.

Country party: ask the children to come to the party dressed as the country of their choice. They could come in the typical traditional dress, or they could wear a mixture of costume and objects from the country of their choice, e.g a bit of garlic around the neck, a stripey T-shirt, a beret, a neckerchief (for France).
Film or televison character party
Circus party

Name Game set to rhythm
• • • •

Set up as for usual Name Game (see *Party Games* on page 9). Instead of counting out the beat of four, do two claps and two finger clicks. Work that into a rhythm with the children. Then you move around the circle with everyone saying their names. But they can only say their name on the second click. When everyone has mastered this, speed up the rhythm.

Additional Checklist

☆ An object for *Changing Object* game

☆ Ten anagrams written on paper

☆ Advert suggestions

☆ Chair

☆ Dressing-up clothes and props

☆ Large bowl

☆ Two sheets of paper for everyone

☆ Enough pens for everyone or enough for sharing

Give Me that Chair

• • • •

Place a chair in the middle of the room. Ask one of the children to sit on it. One-by-one, the children must try to persuade the person sitting on the chair to get off without touching them. They can say things like 'The house is on fire', 'I'm one hundred and eight years old', 'That's my chair!' They must think up their own reason to get the person off the chair and the reason can't be repeated. The person on the chair must move if a good case is put to them.

1-2-3

• • • •

Still in the circle, give each child a number, either one, two or three. Make sure there are equal numbers of children for each number. The idea is, you call out a number (e.g number one) and all the people with number ones get up and run in a clockwise direction round the circle. The last person back to their place is 'out' and they have to lie on their tummies.

Chinese Whispers

• • • •

(See *Party Games* on page 9).

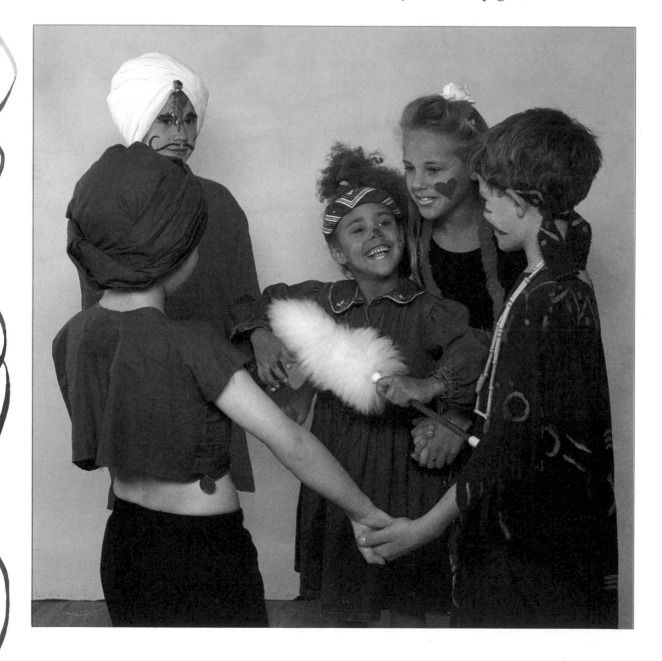

Spot the Ad
• • • •

Split the children into two groups. Give each group a card with the name of a current well-known advertisement written on it. Each group must act out their ad without sound. The other group has to guess the ad.

Teatime
• • • •

Try to make the tea a bit more grown-up. Maybe have candles on the table, but do supervise!

Set the Scene
• • • •

Put the children into groups of four or five, give each child a character, set them a scene and tell them how they must start and how they must end up. Try to organize some old dressing-up clothes, face paints and a few props. Give each group an area where they can practise and try to help them. After 10 or 15 minutes, set up a stage area and get them to perform to each other.

Magic Bowl
• • • •

Get everyone to sit in a circle. Give them two pieces of paper each and a pen. Ask them to think of two dares, which they would be prepared to do themselves. All the dares must be placed in a bowl. One at a time, each child takes a dare out of the bowl and does it! Anyone who refuses has to do a forfeit.

Pass the Story
• • • •

Stay in the circle. Starting with the Birthday person, they must utter two sentences to start the story and then pass it on. The story can only go around the circle once.

Dos and Don'ts

YAH! DO make sure your child says 'thank you' to everyone for their present.

YAH! DO make sure you establish your authority within the first five minutes, then you are in business.

YAH! DO keep the pace of the party moving. Try not to have too many dull moments.

OOPS! DON'T let your child open the presents until everyone has gone home. Then make a note of who has given what, so your child can write 'thank you' notes.

YAH! DO relax the children first with a simple activity and a game of introduction (see the party plans). This will help to get them in the party mood!

YAH! DO play quiet games before and after tea.

OOPS! DON'T forget to give plenty of praise when the children are trying hard with games like *Changing Object*.

YAH! DO choose music it's possible to dance to.

OOPS! DON'T forget to book disco equipment a month ahead, if hiring.

OOPS! DON'T forget to draw the curtains and set the scene for the candlelit tea.

Countries Cake

4-egg Victoria sandwich cake mixture (see
    chart on page 22) baked in two 20 cm
    (8 in) sandwich tins
125 g (4 oz) buttercream
125 g (4 oz) apricot glaze (see page 22)
750 g (1½ lb) fondant icing
black, yellow, blue, green and red food
    colourings
1 egg white
1 straw
flags and ribbons

1. Bake the cakes at 180°C (350°F/Gas
Mark 4) for 35-40 minutes. Sandwich the
cakes together with buttercream and place
on a cake board. Brush the cake all over
with apricot glaze.

2. Colour 25 g (1 oz) of the fondant icing
black and 25 g (1 oz) yellow. Take three
125 g (4 oz) pieces of fondant icing and
colour one turquoise, one blue and one
green. Leave 50 g (2 oz) white and colour
the remaining icing red.

3. Mark the cake into six sections and cut a
triangular template to fit one section. Use
this template to cut the icings to shape, as
shown, using egg white to stick the sides
together.

4. For example, ice one section with the
Italian flag; roll out a little red icing, a
slightly larger piece of white icing and the
green piece of icing. Cut a slight curve in
each and press together using egg white to
stick them. Cut to size, using the template,
and gently lift it onto the cake with a
palette knife. Trim off the excess icing at
the base of the cake.

5. Repeat this process using the relevant
colours for each flag (see photograph).
Stick a straw in the centre and place flags
from each country in the top. Arrange ribbons of various colours from the straw to
drape down the sides.

Note
A simpler version of the flags can be made
using food colourings to paint on the
coloured bands.

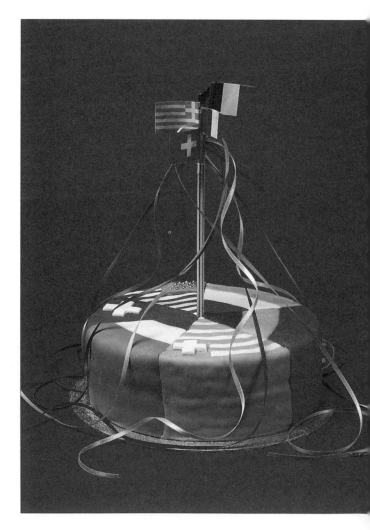

The Great Outdoors

At-a-Glance Party Plan

Name Game

Leapfrog

Do this, Do that . . .

Tag

Chain He

Scavenger Hunt

Outdoor Tea

Pass the Parcel

Limbo Competition

Wheelbarrow Race

Hide 'n' Seek

Fish for Going-home Bags

Children love playing outside on a warm summer day. Unfortunately, parties outside are not as simple as just opening the back door, but, with careful thought and planning, they can be great fun! There are many great games to be played, and the idea of a picnic tea is a tempting treat.

However, careful thought has to be given to the planning of the party. If you are going to have a party outside you will have to have a back-up plan in case it starts to rain or it is unbearably hot. If it is very hot, children start to get extremely grumpy and tearful, and this is when fights and arguments are rife! It is far more comfortable for the children inside in the cool shade of the house.

If you do have the party outside, there are a few safety points you need to bear in mind:

☆ Do make sure that all the children have some form of sun protection on and allocate an adult to keep monitoring the

children's skin. Try to keep them as covered up as possible.

☆ Do have a first aid kit at the ready – somebody is bound to fall over!

☆ If your party is outside in a public place, do make sure you have one adult to every three children, and tell the adult helpers which three children they are to watch over.

☆ If your party is near water, do watch every move the children make. It's possible for small children to drown in a paddling pool. Make sure there are strong adult swimmers in your party.

☆ Do make sure that the party food is not too sticky or the children will end up covered in it, and it will also attract insects.

☆ Don't rely on bouncy castles as your main form of entertainment, the children get bored after a while. Although they are great fun, they must be supervised (there are bound to be a few little bumps). Also, if it starts to rain you are

in trouble if you have nothing else planned.

Name Game

(See *Party Games* on page 9). Start with this game to establish your authority, and also to bring the children together as a group. They will want to run riot outside, so it is a good idea to gain control at the beginning. Play the game in the usual way but, instead of the clapping, use a large beach ball. The ball is thrown around the circle and whoever catches it has to say their name. Make sure everyone has a go.

Leapfrog
●●●●

Arrange the children in two teams. They spread themselves out into two lines with good jumping space between them. Then,

all the children bend over and cuddle up to their knees, keeping their heads tucked well in. The first child in each team then has to leap over the line of children and place themselves in the same position as the rest of the children at the end of the line. The race continues until it is the first child's turn again.

Do this, Do that
• • • •

A great fun game for children. The players freely space themselves out in front of a leader. Whenever she/he says 'Do this' and performs an action, such as stretching arms upwards or clapping hands, all the players must instantly copy them. If, on the other hand, she/he performs an action and says 'Do that' the players must ignore the command and continue doing what they where told to do when the order 'Do that' was given. Anyone who makes a mistake is eliminated. Similarly, if a player does not move quickly enough when 'Do this' is said, that player is also eliminated. The orders should be given very quickly, and the movements should be simple. The game continues until you are left with only one player.

Tag
• • • •

This is a good warm-up game. One person is it, nothing is home. That person has to chase everyone else until they catch someone and then that person becomes It.

Additional Checklist

List of items to find for the Scavenger
Hunt
☆
Beach ball
☆
Pass the Parcel
☆
Broomstick and two chairs for Limbo
Competition
☆
If fishing for going-home bags, home-
made fishing rod and large box

Chain He
••••

Again one person is It, nothing is home.
That person has to try to catch someone else.
As soon as they do, those two players join
hands. Together they have to try to catch the
other players. As each person is caught they
join onto the chain. At the end of the game
you are left with one long chain of children.

Scavenger Hunt
••••

Give the children a list of objects to find,
then let everyone roam around the garden
searching for their treasures, and doing
their own thing! As soon as everyone has
arrived, give them a few minutes, so everyone has a chance to have a good old search
and then gather them together. Make everyone a winner.

*Suggested objects children could search for in
the garden:*
☆ Fallen petal
☆ Feather
☆ Three different types of twig

Outdoor Tea
• • • •

This can be as informal as you like – either sitting on a rug on the grass or use the garden furniture.

Pass the Parcel
• • • •

(See *Party Games* on page 9).

Limbo Competition
• • • •

Place a broomstick on two chairs and arrange the children in a line. One by one, they must pass under the stick, without using their hands. You can make the stick lower and lower, if there is time. Anyone who falls over, or knocks the stick over is out.

Wheelbarrow Race

● ● ● ●

Divide the players into pairs. One player lies on their stomach with their hands to the ground, the other picks up and holds their legs. Set up a small race track and let the players race down it, on hearing your starting whistle.

Hide 'n' Seek

● ● ● ●

Choose one person to be the seeker. That player counts out loud to 30 while the rest of the players hide. The seeker then hunts for those hiding.

If and when, the seeker finds someone, they join the seeker in the hunt for the other players.

Fish for Going-home Bags

● ● ● ●

Set up a large box full of going-home bags. One by one each player has a turn at 'fishing out' their bag. Make a small fishing rod, using a small garden cane, string and a cup hook. Alternatively, hide the bags around the garden. Explain it is one bag per person!

Hallowe'en Parties

Hallowe'en is a great theme for a party, especially for older children – younger ones can get scared if the costumes are too good! This theme provides lots of scope for games, activities and food. For this party, I have assumed that the children are a mixture of ages, from five upwards.

Hallowe'en costumes are very easy to make – in fact the children can design and make them themselves. The following are a few ideas for costumes:

Witch: most girls want to be a witch at Hallowe'en parties. This costume is very easy-to-make. You will need some black card. Cut the card into a square shape, then roll it around into a cone large enough to fit the child's head. Cut off the excess to make the bottom of the cone level all the way round. Secure the cone with glue and sticky tape. Place the cone on another square of black card, draw around the base of the cone and cut out the circle so your child's head can fit through. Then cut out a larger circle to make the brim of the hat and secure it with glue and sticky tape. To decorate, cut out star and moon shapes from silver foil and stick them onto the hat. Finally find some black clothes – tights, a large black T-shirt and something for a witch's cape, such as a black dustbin liner or a large black shawl. If you have a garden broom use that as a witch's broom, if not, then a toy cat or scary animal can then act as their creepy assistant!

Wizard: this costume is much the same as the witch's, the only thing you need to change is the colour. If you can, use purple but any colour will do. You can then give the child a special wizardy-type name to go with their choice of colour, for example the Yellow Wizard of Yellonga.

Black Cat: the child needs a black leotard and tights, some ears glued onto a hair band, and a black tail (sew a long tube of thick material, stuff if liked and pin or sew to outfit). As a final touch, paint on some whiskers.

Ghost: you need an old white sheet or table-cloth. Cut out holes for the eyes and mouth and paint a rim around the holes

in black paint. Pop it over your child's head and you have an instant scary ghost costume.

Devil costume: this requires a little bit more work. You need a red leotard and tights, a tail with an arrow at the end and a fork to hold. Paint on a red face and a black pointy chin.

Other ideas could include a skeleton, mummie, ghoul, monster, Dracula, pumpkin, spider, cobweb.

Invitations
• • • •

To keep to the theme and set the party scene, you can make easy Hallowe'en invitations. All you need is a sheet of black card. Make a very simple template of a bat and cut out enough bats to make invitations for everyone. Then with a silver pen (available from most large stationers), fill in your party details.

Decorations

• • • •

No Hallowe'en party would be complete without a pumpkin carved into the shape of a Jack O'Lantern. All you need is a large pumpkin, with the middle scooped out (the flesh can be used for soup). On the outside of the pumpkin simply carve out two triangle shapes for eyes, a rectangular nose and a larger shape for the mouth. Then place a candle or a nightlight inside (see page 62).

Good traditional colours for Hallowe'en decorations are orange and black. Pin plastic skeletons, bats, spiders and so on all around the party room (then they act as going-home presents). If you have enough black card, you can cut out silhouettes of black cats, bats and witches. You can also make your own ghost. All you need is a balloon and a large white cloth. Attach the balloon to the centre of the cloth and drape the cloth over it, draw black circles for the eyes and mouth, then hang it from the ceiling.

Decorating Bats

• • • •

Prepare a table with a bat for each child. As they arrive, give them a little rubber or card bat each and then ask them to set about personalizing their own bat. They must also think of a pet name for it. When they have all finished and the bats are all completely dry, they can be placed in the going-home bags.

Name Game

• • • •

(See *Party Games* on page 9). The children must introduce themselves as the character they are dressed up as and tell a bit about themselves. If anyone is shy, ask them a few questions to encourage them, but don't push them.

Monster Musical Statues

• • • •

(See *Party Games* on page 9). Find some good old-fashioned, scary music. (Michael Jackson's *Thriller* is a good one for this game.) Every time the music stops, the children have to stop in the position of the statue you call out. Each time, make it a bit more scary. Suggested statues include witch's cat, ghost, wizard, mummie, witch, vampire.

Apple Bobbing

• • • •

Spread a large plastic sheet over the floor. You then need a large bowl full of water and an apron. Float some apples in the water –

Additional Checklist

☆ Rubber or paper bats (enough for everyone)

☆ Glue, glitter and fun paper for decorating bats

☆ Scary party music

☆ Apples enough for everyone, with a few spare

☆ Large bowl with water

☆ Plastic sheet (bin bag will do)

☆ Large bowl with lid and seven objects to fill it

☆ Pencil and paper

☆ Torch

☆ String to make a washing line to hang buns

☆ Buns (enough for everyone)

leave the stalks on as this makes it easier. One-by-one, the children, with their hands behind their backs, must kneel down and take an apple out of the water.

Witch's Cauldron
• • • •

Take a large bowl or saucepan with a lid and fill it with about seven objects. One by one, the children put their hands inside the cauldron and feel inside. As each child goes to take their turn, the lights must be turned off. After their turn, the lights go back on and the child quickly writes down what they felt. Try to put a time limit on everyone. Suggested objects: rubber glove, sponge, small furry toy.

Scary Storytelling
• • • •

All the children must sit in a circle. Together they tell a scary story. Each child is only allowed to utter three sentences and then the story is passed onto the next person. The children must listen carefully so they can add their piece!

Musical Torch
• • • •

This is a musical passing game. The children stay seated in their circle. Music plays and a torch is passed around hand-to-hand, held under the chin so that each child's face is lit up in a very scary manner. Whoever is holding the torch when the music stops has to lie on their tummy. The game continues until there is only one person left sitting – the winner!

Buns on-the-Line
• • • •

Hang one small bun for each child (if there is room) on a long string. The children then have to eat the hanging buns without touching them with their hands – their hands must be behind their backs. If there is not enough room for everyone you can play the game in groups.

Apples under the Chin
• • • •

Divide the children into two teams. The team members stand behind each other in lines. Each team is given an apple. The apple must be passed down the line, under the chins (without hands, again). When the apple gets to the bottom of the line, the last person takes the apple and joins the front of the line. This is repeated until the person who started at the head of the queue returns.

Going-home Bags
• • • •

Bring out that old cauldron again. But this time fill it with party bags.

Troubleshooting

However organized you are and however carefully you plan your party, there will always be a hitch somewhere along the line. Remember that you are dealing with children! Nothing will be so bad that you can't handle it, just don't panic. The following are a few of the problems that might occur.

The birthday person
• • • •

At all costs try to keep your child calm before the party. Give them little jobs to do to keep their mind off the party, or better still if there is a grown-up around who can take the child out for a while that would be great. If the child is too excited, they will

either become very shy or totally out of control during the whole of the party. Most of the partygoers will take their lead from the birthday child, so if the birthday child is shy or over-excited, the rest of the party guests will follow suit.

The birthday child's brothers and sisters

Try to make them 'special' too. But make sure that they know whose birthday it is. Give them little jobs to do during the party (handing around drinks, looking after younger children). This way they feel part of the action. Give them a small 'unbirthday' present as a thank you.

Parties of mixed ages/family parties

• • • •

These can sometimes be quite difficult. Always ask the older children to be helpers, that way they don't feel they are being treated like a baby and they will enjoy the party

much more and won't be difficult. Aim the party at the average age group and get the adults to join in as much as possible.

Latecomers

• • • •

Children who arrive late always feel awful. Involve them very quietly in whatever you are doing, without drawing too much attention to them, otherwise they will want the floor to open up!

Shy children

• • • •

If a child is shy, don't try to force them, they will simply get worse. First, find someone who knows them well and arrange for them to sit together. Don't make too much of a fuss. They usually don't want any attention but just want to merge into the background. If you make too much of a fuss then the rest of the children will side with the shy child and you will have everyone

refusing to join in. Games like *Pass the Parcel* are great for 'breaking the ice', because the shy child can be part of everything, without actually 'joining-in'. If a child is painfully shy, don't stop the parcel on them. That way they are not put on the spot. You often find that a child who is shy to start off with becomes the most extrovert by the end of the party!

Refusing to join in

If a child refuses to join in, don't just let them sit there. Make them a judge or involve them in some other way. If the children see a child sitting out watching they will want to join them.

Distraught children

If a child arrives in floods of tears, clinging to a parent, ask the parent to stay while the child settles in. Try to get the parent to join in with everything, that way the child will gradually become a part of things. If the parent has to leave, take their telephone number.

Over-eager children

If you find yourself swamped with children who all want to help, all you have to say is 'I willl choose the person who is sitting with their legs crossed, arms folded and a big smile.' You will be surprised how this will work wonders.

Over-excited children

You soon know which are the high-spirited children. The best way to deal with them is try not to get cross. Normally, what seems like bad behaviour is pure excitement, so try to be patient. The golden rule is be firm but fair. If one child is being really troublesome – hitting other children, throwing things, ignoring everything you say, then it is a good idea to get them to move into another room away from the fun for a while. Don't get cross, just take them into the kitchen with one of the adult helpers, where they can hear the other children still having a good time and this will usually make them calm down. If someone is really uncontrollable just call their parents.

Fights

Don't allow any fighting – not even play fights. In my experience party play fights always end in tears. Again, it's all down to good old excitement. Someone will get carried away and hurt someone else and all hell will break loose. If a fight breaks out, change the activity to a much, much quieter one, such as *Sleeping Lions*.

Accidents

If an accident happens at the party you must always tell the parents. This way they will know exactly what is wrong if the child feels ill later on. Have plenty of plasters at the ready. Do not give any of the children medication, no matter how ill they feel.

If they really are unwell, call the parents. If an accident does occur, don't panic, take the children away and arrange for an adult to deal with the injured child. If there is a head injury of any kind, a deep puncture to the skin, or a really bad knock then the child should go to the casualty department of your local hospital.

They won't eat the food

••••

Sometimes children will just look at the food but won't touch it, no matter what you do! Always make sure that you have worn them out a bit with activities first. If this doesn't work, then let them drink a bit and eat a little, and play some more games. Then come back to the food later. Make sure that you put all the savoury things out first. If they see lots of lovely sweet things the savoury things will be left behind! Try to dissuade the children from over-filling their plates; this will stop them eating properly. Children's eyes are always bigger than their tummies. Make sure that someone is around to help them while they are eating as this will stop any food throwing and misbehaviour. The children need to be supervised at all times, do not leave them for a minute.

Do's and Don'ts

YAH! DO make sure that all balloons are tied up out of the reach of the children. If an excitable child pulls the whole lot down, take them away. Balloons can cause havoc. Everyone will want the blue one and there will be tears and fights over it! The same will happen with any loose hanging decorations. It will only take one child to pull a streamer down and that will be enough to start a riot.

YAH! DO make sure you stick to your party plan. There is more than enough material for each age group in the party plans in this book, with plenty to spare should the games go too quickly.

YAH! DO ensure that you go through the checklists and have everything close to hand in your party prop box.

YAH! DO establish your authority. If the children know the rules and you are firm about them (without being a spoilsport) they will respect you. If you don't set the rules, be warned!

OOPS! DON'T let anybody refuse to join. Children are herd animals, they will all copy each other. Try a simple test: cough in front of a group of children and see what happens – you will be surprised!

OOPS! DON'T have the parents in the same area as the children. They will talk louder than you (without thinking), and if their child is being naughty they will either discipline them and make a scene, or they will sit there and watch their child wreck your house without a word, and you can't really rebuke the child if the parent doesn't.

OOPS! DON'T start any games until everyone is ready. It is hard to get everyone involved, and if you start a game without explaining the rules to all the children, the ones that missed out will either wander off or become disruptive. So, before each game, sit them down and explain the rules.

Useful Address Book

ENTERTAINERS
••••
London

Spotty Dotty (alias Amanda Muden the author),
Tel. 0181 540 4728, 01956 409322
Captain Dick, Tel. 0171 258 0128
Comedygrams, Tel. 0181 399 6007
Mr Gee,
Tel. 0181 678 6908, 01956 233376
Nutty Nellie, Tel. 0181 340 5972
Peter Pinner Entertainments,
Tel. 0181 863 1528
Tony Hollis, Tel. 0181 341 3487
Twizzle Entertainments, Tel. 0181 748 3138
Uncle Jack and Johnny Sunshine,
Tel. 0181 678 6909

South East England

Crazy Chris,
Tel. 01784 453192, 01850 461543
Mr McDonut,
Tel. 01932 847464, 01860 6155912

South West England

Colonel Mustard, Tel. 01296 434727
Magician Adair, Tel. 01271 79914
Magical Mikey,
Tel. 01844 345787, 01850 959189
Reg Webb Entertainments,
Tel. 01494 873194

North West England

Pepe the Clown and Company,
Tel. 01253 714278

Scotland

Magic Bob, Tel. 01573 410363

FACE PAINTING
••••

Creative Faces - can supply top quality face painters and temporary tattoo artistes anywhere in the UK
Tel. 0181 444 4489, 01956 260148

Face paint suppliers
Creative Faces - stock a full range of theatrical and water based make-up (as used in the book) - Ellington Place, 10 Ellington Road, London N10 3DG

PARTY SERVICES / SUPPLIERS
••••

Puddleduck Parties - complete party packages delivered to your door - from food and entertainment to equipment and going home gifts. Themes a speciality.
Tel. 0171 351 0432
The Kite and Balloon Emporium Limited,
613 Garratt Lane, London SW18 4SU
Tel. 0181 946 5962
The Non-Stop Party Shop,
214-216 Kensington High Street, London W8 7RG
Tel. 0171 937 7200
Frog Hollow,
15 Victoria Grove, London W8 5RW
Tel. 0171 581 5493
Paperchase,
213 Tottenham Court Road, London
Tel. 0171 580 8496
Party Props - mini bouncy castles, ball ponds, tunnels and bubble machines; also provides children's tables and chairs. Bookings and information
Tel. 0181 946 8769
IKEA - puppet theatre
Tel. 0181 451 5566

Acknowledgements

The Author and Publishers would like to thank the following
for all their help with this book:

Jilly Henderson, Joan O'Toole, Gabriella Ramacciotti (stylist), Buffer Bears Nursery in
Wimbledon and all the little friends who agreed to be photographed.
Phil of Creative Faces for the brilliant step-by-step face painting.
The Kite and Balloon Emporium Limited, Frog Hollow,
The Non-Stop Party Shop, Paperchase, Movie Mites.